Mind Your Manners,
Dick and Jane

GROSSET & DUNLAP
Published by the Penguin Group
Penguin Group (USA) Inc., 375 Hudson Street, New York, New York 10014, U.S.A.
Penguin Group (Canada), 90 Eglinton Avenue East, Suite 700,
Toronto, Ontario, Canada M4P 2Y3
(a division of Pearson Penguin Canada Inc.)
Penguin Books Ltd, 80 Strand, London WC2R 0RL, England
Penguin Ireland, 25 St Stephen's Green, Dublin 2, Ireland
(a division of Penguin Books Ltd)
Penguin Group (Australia), 250 Camberwell Road, Camberwell, Victoria 3124, Australia
(a division of Pearson Australia Group Pty Ltd)
Penguin Books India Pvt Ltd, 11 Community Centre,
Panchsheel Park, New Delhi - 110 017, India
Penguin Group (NZ), Cnr Airborne and Rosedale Roads, Albany, Auckland 1310, New Zealand
(a division of Pearson New Zealand Ltd)
Penguin Books (South Africa) (Pty) Ltd, 24 Sturdee Avenue, Rosebank,
Johannesburg 2196, South Africa

Penguin Books Ltd, Registered Offices:
80 Strand, London WC2R 0RL, England

Designed by Shane Breaux

Dick and Jane™ is a trademark of Pearson Education, Inc. Text copyright © 2006 by Pearson
Education, Inc. Various illustrations © by Scott, Foresman and Company: *Before We Read* ©
1951; *Fun Wherever We Are* © 1962, renewed 1990; *Fun with Dick and Jane* © 1940; *Fun with
Our Friends* © 1962; *Guess Who* © 1951, renewed 1979; *The New Fun with Dick and Jane* © 1956,
renewed 1984; *The New Guess Who* © 1965, renewed 1993; *Our New Friends* © 1940, renewed
1968; *We Come and Go* © 1940, renewed 1968; *We Look and See* © 1946, renewed 1974; *We Read
More Pictures* © 1951, renewed 1979; *We Work and Play* © 1951, 1946, 1940. Illustrations ©
by Pearson Education, Inc.: *A Christmas Story* © 2004. Reprinted by permission of Pearson
Education, Inc. All rights reserved. Published in 2006 by Grosset & Dunlap, a division of
Penguin Young Readers Group, 345 Hudson Street, New York, New York 10014. GROSSET &
DUNLAP is a trademark of Penguin Group (USA) Inc. Printed in the U.S.A.

Library of Congress Cataloging-in-Publication Data

Ostow, Micol.
Mind your manners, Dick and Jane / by Micol Ostow and Noah Harlan.
p. cm.
ISBN 0-448-44433-X (hardcover)
1. Etiquette for children and teenagers. I. Harlan, Noah. II. Title.
BJ1857.C5O88 2006
395.1'22—dc22   2006011383

10 9 8 7 6 5 4 3 2 1

Mind Your Manners, Dick and Jane

By *Micol Ostow and Noah Harlan*

Grosset & Dunlap

Table of Contents

Introduction

See Dick and Jane.
See Dick and Jane eat dinner.

Jane is talking with her mouth
full of food.
Dick is speaking on his cell phone.
What is Sally doing?
Sally is feeding Spot.
Spot is begging for more food.

Jane, close your mouth
while you are chewing!
Dick, do not use your cell phone
at the dinner table!
Sally, do not feed the dog
from the table!
Mind your manners!
Mind your manners, Dick and Jane!

*W*hat are manners? Manners are a way of being kind, courteous, and respectful toward one another. Manners—good and bad—can affect everything that we do, from how we talk to others to how we dress to how we behave in public.

We all should practice good manners whenever we can. But sometimes—like Dick and Jane—we forget.

Come with Dick and Jane as they learn proper behavior in any situation. We will learn all about modern manners. Oh, the fun we'll have!

PART I

HOME AND FAMILY

Communication

See Dick.
Dick is reading.
Read, Dick, read.

Sally would like to play.
Dick does not want
to play right now.
"Right now, I am reading."

Sally is angry.
She would like to play.
She shouts at Dick.
Now Dick is angry, too.

*B*eing part of a family can be hard work! People in our family do not always want to do what we want to do, *when* we want to do it. But it's important to always speak to people in a respectful tone of voice, whether it's our mother, father, sister, or brother.

Always remember the Golden Rule of manners: *Do unto others as you would have them do unto you.*

Pop Quiz

Your younger brother wants to watch the football game on TV, but you are watching your favorite sitcom. Do you:

(a) Shout at your brother and toss the remote control across the room?

(b) Storm out of the room in anger?

(c) Tattle to your parents that your brother is bothering you?

(d) Explain to him that you are watching your own TV show right now, but offer to let him have some time in front of the TV in a little while?

Answer Key The answer is (d), of course! Answers (a), (b), and (c) are just plain rude.

Chores

See Dick.
Dick is playing on his computer.
Play, Dick, play.

See Sally.
Sally is washing dishes.
Wash, Sally, wash.

Dick was supposed to help
Sally with the dishes.
Dick was going to dry.
But Dick is busy playing.
Now Sally will have to
wash and dry by herself.

See Sally sulk.

*I*n most households, each member of the family has his or her own chores to do. You might be in charge of walking the dog, while your brother or sister takes out the trash.

It's important to stay on top of your chores. If not, you are making more work for someone else. And that's not very considerate at all.

Managing Relationships

See Dick.
Dick likes computers.

See Sally.
Sally likes dolls.

Sally wants someone to play
dolls with her.
Dick wants someone to play
computer games with him.

What will they do?
It is easy—Sally will play
computer games with Dick.
Dick will play dolls with Sally.

Now everyone is happy!
Play, Dick and Sally, play!

*I*n any household, compromise is key. Sometimes you will have to give a little to get a little. Maybe tonight your mother is making your sister's favorite dinner. That doesn't seem fair, now, does it? But tomorrow she will make something that you like.

The important thing is to always be as patient and understanding as you possibly can.

Sharing, Borrowing, and Lending

See Sally.
Sally is going to a party.
She wants to wear
something special.

See Sally borrow Mother's
earrings—without permission.
Bad idea, Sally.
See Sally get grounded.

It's important to always respect people's possessions. If you wish to borrow something that belongs to someone else, you must ask permission. Sometimes permission will be granted. Sometimes it will not. That's just the way it goes.

When it comes to lending, it's nice to be generous. But you don't always have to lend out your belongings if you don't feel comfortable doing so. It's up to you!

Dos and Don'ts for a Happy Household

DO		DON'T
Be respectful of others.	*	*Throw temper tantrums.*
Clean up after yourself.	*	*Expect your mother to pick up after you.*
Your homework.	*	*Do your sister's or brother's homework.*
Share your toys.	*	*Share your toothbrush.*

PART II

TABLE MANNERS

Family Meals at Home

See Jane.
See Sally.
Where is Dick?
He is not there!

What is that noise?
Is it Dick?
No, it is Jane's and Sally's
tummies rumbling.
Jane and Sally are oh so hungry.
The food is getting cold.
Dick is late.
Late, late, late . . .

*I*t is important to be polite to others—including members of your family. Dick is late, and Jane and Sally have to wait for him. This is not polite. This is not good manners. Jane and Sally are waiting for Dick before they start. This is very polite. This is good manners. Don't be late!

Setting the Table

See Dick.
Dick is setting the table.
"May I help you, Dick?" asks Jane.
"Yes, please!" says Dick.
"You can lay the silverware
out on the table."
"Okay!" says Jane.

See Jane set the table.
"Oh, Jane!" Dick says.
"Not in one big pile!"
See Dick shake his head.
Shake, shake, shake . . .

*D*ick and Jane are being very helpful because Mother and Father are very busy. It is always good manners to help your parents prepare for a meal. Jane has just learned how to set a table. There is an order to how we arrange a place setting:

bread plate

glass

plate

fork

knife   spoon

Serving the Food

See Dick.
See Jane.
See food on Dick's plate.
Jane does not have her food yet.

Put your fork down, Dick!
That is not polite!
People will think
you are a little piglet!

See Dick wait until everyone
has been served.
That is better, Dick.
That is better.

*P*atience is a virtue! Patience is also good manners. When eating a meal with others, be they friends or family, always wait until everyone has been served before starting your food. If you are serving yourself, do not take too much. Leave enough for everyone. Yum!

Eating the Meal

See Dick.
See Jane.
See Dick and Jane eating dinner.

"How was your day, Dick?"
asks Jane.
"It wasz sho good."
Why does Dick not make sense?
Because Dick's mouth is full of
food!

Chew and swallow, Dick!
Chew and swallow!

See Jane reach for more peas.
Oh no, Jane! Look out!
See Jane's sleeve in Dick's soup.

*D*ick and Jane are displaying very bad table manners. Always chew with your mouth closed, and never speak before you swallow your food. If you would like something from the table, ask someone to please pass it— and be sure to say *thank you.*

Believe it or not, sometimes it is good manners to eat with your hands! But sometimes it is not. Here is a chart to help you.

FINGER FOOD		USE UTENSILS
Chicken wings	*	*Chicken breast*
Hamburger	*	*T-bone steak*
Potato chips	*	*Mashed potatoes*
Sandwich	*	*Stew*

Clearing After Dinner

See the table.
There is nothing on it!
Where did the meal go?

After the meal, Dick and Jane
cleared their plates.
Go, go, Dick and Jane!
You have mastered table manners!

Helpful Hints for Tricky Dishes

TRICKY DISH	HELPFUL HINT
Soup	Never slurp your soup. Never drink from the bowl.
Asparagus	Asparagus can be eaten with your hands, but only if they are short stalks! Never use the "spears" to poke your friends!
Lobster	Put on a bib or hang a napkin from your neck. This way, you will leave the dinner table looking nice and neat! Use the little, tiny fork to get the meat from the claws. Yum!
Fat and gristly bits of meat	Don't spit tough-to-chew pieces onto your plate. Bring your napkin to your mouth, and put the meat into the napkin. Then you can place it on the edge of your plate. Never feed it to the dog!
Artichoke	Take the leaves, one at a time, and scrape them with your two front teeth. When you have just the center left, eat it with a knife and fork.

PART III

PUBLIC BEHAVIOR

Your Appearance

Grooming

See Dick.
See Dick's shirt.
It is not tucked in.
It is also wrinkled.

See Dick's hair.
He has not brushed it today.

Dick is eating chocolate.
It is smeared across his cheek.

Dick is very messy!
That is not good manners.

Clean up, Dick.
Scrub, scrub, scrub . . .

*H*aving good manners is more than what you say—
it is also how you appear. For instance, it is not
considered good manners to appear sloppy or slovenly.

If you are going out in public, be sure to take a bath or
shower beforehand. Brush your teeth and your hair, and
choose clothes that are appropriate for wherever you will be
that day.

Dressing for Different Occasions

Today is class picture day.
Smile for the camera.
Smile, Dick!
Smile, Jane!
Smile and say cheese.

Teacher is not smiling.
She is upset with Jane.

Jane is wearing sweat pants.
The other students are wearing
dress clothes.
Jane's outfit does NOT look good
for picture day.
She is ruining the picture for all
of her classmates.
That is not polite.

*D*ifferent occasions call for different types of outfits. For instance, sneakers are a good thing to wear if you are playing a sport, but *not* if you are going to church. In church you should wear a dress or slacks, but not sunglasses or blue jeans. Sunglasses are for the park, the beach, or the swimming pool. Blue jeans are for the weekend, or for just hanging around.

It's important to always dress for the occasion!

Diet and Exercise

Today Dick is going
to a birthday party.
He will eat lots of cake
and ice cream.
Yum, yum, yum!

But—uh-oh!
Dick has eaten too many sweets.
Now he has a stomachache.
Ow, ow, ow.
Stomachaches are no fun.

*A*s we have learned, it is important to take care of yourself on the outside by washing, brushing your hair and teeth, and dressing nicely. But it is important to take care of yourself on the inside, too. This means making sure to eat healthy—at least most of the time. Sweets and treats are okay, but do not go overboard. And be sure to get plenty of exercise, too! Exercise will help to keep your body fit and strong.

HEALTHY CHOICE		UNHEALTHY CHOICE
Fruit salad	*	*Gummi cherries*
Milk	*	*Milk chocolate*
Playing outside	*	*Watching too much TV*

Sleep

"Time to clean up," Mother says.
"Time to get ready for bed."
"I do not want to go to bed!"
  Dick says.
  He stomps his foot.
  Stomp, stomp, stomp.

Dick is tired.
Dick is being cranky.

It is no fun to have to go to sleep when there are so many other exciting things to do!

But bedtimes are set for a reason. When we don't get enough sleep, we can be grouchy and unpleasant. And no one wants to play with someone who is grouchy and unpleasant!

Your Presentation

Body Language and Posture

See Dick.
Dick runs in the house.
Run, Dick, run!
Crash, crash, crash.
Uh-oh.

Dick has knocked over
Mother's favorite plant.
Mother is cross.
She does not say anything.
How does Dick know that
Mother is cross?
He can tell from her body language.

*B*ody language is what your movements and gestures communicate to other people. For instance, if you are angry, you may cross your arms over your chest. If you are exasperated, you may place your hands on your hips.

People can tell a lot about your mood simply from your body language. Therefore, you should be aware of your body language whenever you can. Try to stand up straight and look people in the eye. This tells people that you are confident, friendly, and outgoing. If you are feeling grumpy, just remember: Turn your frown upside down!

Frown

Smile

Personal Space

See Dick.
Dick is on the playground.
He is waiting for the slide.

Uh-oh.
Right now someone else
is using the slide.
The boys and girls are
all waiting in line.

But not Dick.
Dick is impatient.
Dick pushes to the front.
He squishes up against
the other boys and girls.
Do not squish, Dick!
Do not squish!

*I*t is not polite to cut in line the way that Dick did. It is also not polite to squish up against people in a way that makes them uncomfortable or crowds them. Everyone prefers to have his or her own personal space. For instance, when you talk to someone, be sure to stand or sit at least a few paces apart from him or her.

Speech and Enunciation

See Jane.
Jane is meeting a friend
of Mother's.
"Hello, Jane," Mother's friend says.

Jane looks at the ground.
She is feeling shy.
She replies very quietly.

Mother's friend cannot hear Jane.
"What is that?" she asks.
Do not mumble, Jane!
Do not mumble.
Mumbling is impolite.

$\mathcal{E}$veryone feels shy sometimes, and we don't always feel like talking to others. But it's impolite not to answer when people ask us questions. We must speak up clearly so that we can be understood. Make sure not to cover your mouth when you are having a conversation. Let them see those pearly whites!

Speaking clearly is called *enunciating.*

Enunciating is good manners.

Making Conversation

See Dick.
Dick is at dinner with his family
and some friends.
There are many people sitting
at the table.
Lots of people are talking at once.
Dick would like to talk, too.
But Dick is too shy.
Speak up, Dick! Speak up.

*S*ometimes we spend time by ourselves, and sometimes we spend time in groups.

Large groups can be intimidating. Sometimes we don't know what to say or how to join a conversation.

If you would like to talk to people, it is a good idea to ask them questions about themselves. You could ask them what books they like to read or what their hobbies are. People will be pleased that you have taken an interest in them.

If you know you are going to be at a dinner or a party, you might want to come up with some conversation topics beforehand. Good conversation topics are lighthearted and not too personal. For instance, you could tell people about a funny thing that happened to you at school recently. People love funny stories!

When it comes to making conversation, practice makes perfect.

Talking to Adults

Knock, knock, knock!
Who is that knocking at the door?
Who can it be?
How very exciting.
We have a guest!
See Jane answer the door.

"Hello, Mrs. Kerfluffle.
How are you today?" asks Jane.

"I am fine, thank you.
Is your mother at home?"

"Yes, she is.
I will go get her for you
right away, ma'am."

*W*hen talking to adults, you should always be polite. It is always nice to be helpful and courteous. When adults are talking to each other, sit quietly and don't interrupt. It's rude to interrupt! Rude, rude, rude . . .

Dinner Parties

Look at all the people.
The house is so full!
Mother and Father must
be having a party!

See Jane.
What are you doing, Jane?
Do not take the last piece of cake!
Leave it for somebody else.

See Dick.
Do not stick your carrot back
in the dip!
Do not double dip, Dick.
Do not double dip!

*D*inner parties can be fun and exciting! The house is full of people, and everyone is so happy! Remember to make a good impression and to not make a scene. Your parents are very busy, so you must behave! Talk to the nice adults. Make sure there is enough food, and always let your guests eat first.

Family Gatherings

See Dick and Jane.
See all their distant relatives.

Who is that with the funny hat?
That is Aunt Myrtle!

Who is that with the funny hair?
That is Cousin Buck!

Who is that talking to Jane?
Uh-oh! She does not know!

"I have not seen you since you
were born," says the woman.

"It is so nice to see you!"
says Jane.

Smile and nod, Jane.
Smile and nod.

amily gatherings can be lots of fun. Weddings, reunions, birthdays, and holidays! Sometimes, if you have a big family, you may not remember everyone—even if they remember you! It is okay not to remember someone. Smile and be polite; tell them it is nice to see them again. You can also apologize and say that you don't remember meeting them. That's okay! You are very young and have met so many people!

Religious Events

See Dick.
See Jane.
They are in church.

See Dick and Jane sitting
quietly and listening.
See Dick and Jane dressed
in their Sunday best.
What a lovely suit you have, Dick.
What a pretty dress you have, Jane.

All across the world, people practice many different religions. If you are going to a religious event, you must be sure to practice good manners. Wear nice clothes. No blue jeans in there! Make sure to bathe and comb your hair. And of course, leave your magazines, cell phones, and iPods at home!

At School

See Jane.
Jane is in class.

See Teacher.
Teacher is teaching.

What is Jane doing?
Jane is passing a note
to her friend!
Bad Jane.
Bad, bad, bad.

See Dick.
Dick is in class, too!
Dick is paying attention.
Dick is going to get an A+!
You go, Dick!

School is very important for boys and girls. You can learn many wonderful things. Even if you don't like every subject, you should always pay attention and try your best. Don't distract others—they are trying to learn, too! There is plenty of time after school to play with your friends, but not during class. Also, be respectful of your teachers. They work very hard to help you be successful!

Out and About

Public Events and Spaces

See Dick.
See Jane.
They are watching a movie.

Do you wonder what it could be?
Maybe an action movie.
Maybe an animated movie.
Maybe a postmodern film noir!

See Dick share his popcorn with Jane.
That is nice of you, Dick.

What is that noise?
Oh no, it is the people behind them.
They are talking during the movie!
That is not nice at all.

*P*ublic events can be a lot of fun. Movies and concerts and theater, oh boy! Remember that there are many people in a public space—whether it is for a performance or on a bus! Be considerate—don't disturb the people around you. If you are watching a movie or performance, don't talk until it is over. If you are in a public place, such as a restaurant or an elevator, you may talk, but keep your voice down.

Trips and Travel

See Dick and Jane.
See Dick and Jane in the car.
Where are they going?
They are going to Nana's house!
Oh, what a long trip it is!

What is Dick doing?
See Dick kicking the
back of Father's seat.
Wow, that is really annoying.
Stop that, Dick!

What is Jane doing?
Jane is quietly reading.
Jane knows that it is important to
practice manners, wherever you are.
You go, Jane!

*I*t is great to go on vacation with family and friends—but you should never take a vacation from good manners! When traveling, either in a car, a plane, or a hotel room, you'll be spending a lot of time with others in very close quarters. This can be stressful. When en route to your destination, try to keep to yourself and keep your voice to a minimum. Rowdy behavior might be fun for you, but it is very unpleasant for others.

You can come up with some quiet ways to amuse yourself—*before* you hit the road:

Good and Bad Activities on a Trip

GOOD		BAD
Playing "I Spy"	*	*Playing "Tag"*
Reading to yourself	*	*Reading out loud*
Listening to your headphones	*	*Singing out loud with your headphones*

Jobs

See Dick.
He has a job!
Dick is selling lemonade.

See Jane.
Jane is thirsty.

"How may I help you, Jane?"
says Dick.

"I am so thirsty. May I please
have a glass of lemonade?"
"Of course," says Dick. "That
will be twenty-five cents."

See Jane pay Dick.

Congratulations, Dick!
You just made a quarter!

*H*aving a job is a very big responsibility. You have to show up on time and work very hard, or you may not have a job much longer. If you have a paper route, people want their newspaper! If you are babysitting, you are responsible for keeping a young child safe and sound! Always be polite and courteous to your customers and coworkers. Groom yourself and dress nicely—nobody wants to buy lemonade from someone who has dirty hands. Be helpful and attentive, and you will go far!

PART IV

SOCIAL SETTINGS

Meeting New People

Today is the first day of school.
See all the children playing in
the classroom.

But wait!
Where is Jane?
Jane is standing in the corner.
She is all by herself.
Jane is shy.

Poor, poor Jane . . .

*E*verybody feels shy at times. It can be overwhelming to meet new people. But it doesn't have to be! When meeting new people, being polite and being yourself are the two biggest steps to remember.

Always introduce yourself. Say hello and state your name clearly. When meeting someone for the first time, it is also good manners to shake his or her hand. A firm handshake is considered confident.

Places for Meeting New People

GOOD		BAD
A big party	*	*The doctor's office*
The school lunchroom	*	*The principal's office*
A playground during recess	*	*A classroom during math class*

Making Friends

See Dick at recess.
Dick is playing tetherball.
He is playing all alone.

Bop goes the ball . . .
Bop goes the ball . . .

Ooh—what are those
other boys doing?
They are playing catch!
Dick would like to play catch, too.
Do not worry, Dick!
You can make friends with
these boys.
Then you can play catch, too.

"Boy, oh boy!" says Dick.
"Let's make friends."

$\mathcal{M}$aking new friends can be overwhelming. But most people, when approached politely, are perfectly friendly.

How can you spot a potential new friend? Well, a new friend is often someone with whom you have something in common. You can start by saying hello and introducing yourself. Then you might comment on a book that he or she is reading, or compliment him or her on a well-played game. Soon, you will find yourself in conversation. Now you are on your way to making a new friend!

Being Polite

See Dick.
Dick is on the playground.
He is watching some
boys play soccer.

Dick points at one
of the players.
Now the soccer players
feel self-conscious.
Do not point, Dick!
Do not point!
Pointing is not polite.

As we have learned, meeting new people and making new friends are not very hard to do. Most people are very outgoing and happy to talk—when they are approached politely, that is.

What is considered polite? Polite is approaching people openly, respecting their space, and not asking too many personal questions.

And remember—never point at or crowd someone. That is considered aggressive behavior, which is very bad manners.

Sportsmanship

It is softball season!
See Jane at bat.
Swing, Jane, swing!

Uh-oh.
Jane has struck out.
Jane tosses her bat
aside and pouts.
Do not pout, Jane!
Do not pout!
Jane is being a bad sport.

Sports and games are lots of fun to play, and we all like to win. That's only natural. A little bit of competition is healthy, but it's important to remember that at the end of the day, it's only a game.

It's not whether you win or lose, it's how you play. And how you play is called sportsmanship. *Sportsmanship* is another word for good manners when you are competing.

GRACEFUL WINNING **GRACELESS WINNING**
Shaking your opponents' hands ✳ *Gloating*

GRACEFUL LOSING **GRACELESS LOSING**
Congratulating your opponent ✳ *Scowling*
on a game well played

You're Invited

Party Time!
See Jane.
Jane is wearing her
best party dress.
She also has her hair in a bow.
Jane looks very pretty.
She is carrying a present.

Where is Jane going?
A birthday party, of course!
Have fun, Jane!
Have fun!

*P*arties are a great way to spend time with our friends and family. At a party we eat yummy food, play games, and laugh. What could be better?

There are a few simple rules to adhere to in order to make party time perfect.

Dos and Don'ts for a Perfect Party

DO		DON'T
RSVP promptly so that your host and hostess can plan for your attendance.	✳	Show up with more guests than were invited without asking your host for permission in advance.
Bring a dish or something to drink.	✳	Bring your pet, your cell phone, or a book to read. The point of a party is to socialize!
Show up on time, especially if a meal is being served. You wouldn't want people to have to wait for you!	✳	Overstay your welcome. Although if you are one of the last people at the party, it's nice to help clean up.

Dating

It is Saturday night.
Dick is all dressed up!
See Dick's shoes.
They sparkle and shine.

Where is Dick going?
Dick is going to a school dance.
He is going with a date.
Oh, the fun they will have!

*W*hen boys and girls like each other as more than friends, they often want to spend time together. This is called dating. A date can be anything from watching a movie to playing a board game. Mostly, a date means just having fun!

The best way to ask someone on a date is to approach him or her casually and ask if they would like to get together sometime. This can be intimidating, but the more you do it, the easier it will be. Keep in mind that just because you have feelings for someone does *not* guarantee that he or she will feel the same.

You should be outgoing on your date, but you should also be polite. Be punctual; say *please* and *thank you*, and ask questions rather than simply talking about yourself. It's always polite to offer to split the bill.

GOOD FIRST DATES		BAD FIRST DATES
A movie	*	*A library*
A concert	*	*A class*
A party	*	*A funeral*

After-School Functions

See Jane.
Jane is wearing
a bright uniform.
She is carrying
pom-poms.
Jane has joined
the pep squad.
G-O, Jane! G-O!

*E*xtracurricular activities are a great way to get involved at school and in your community. Through extracurricular activities, you will learn new skills, meet new people, and sometimes get to know your classmates and your teachers in a different light.

However, you must always mind your manners as you would anywhere else. This includes speaking politely and deferring to the grown-ups in charge. You should also always practice good sportsmanship.

So go ahead—get involved. Oh, what fun it will be!

PART V

COMMUNICATION

Telephone Etiquette

Ring, ring, ring.

See Sally.
See Sally answer the telephone.
"Hello, this is Sally.
Who is calling?"

See Sally listen.
Listen, Sally, listen.

"I am sorry, my parents are not
available now.
May I take a message?"
See Sally write down the
message for Mother.

*T*he telephone is a wonderful modern convenience. But just because you can't see someone, it doesn't mean you can't practice good manners. Always speak clearly and politely. Never give out your personal information over the telephone, and never tell someone if your parents are not home. Simply say that they are not available, and offer to take a message. When taking messages, write the message clearly on a piece of paper.

When placing a phone call, speak clearly, say hello, and ask for the person you would like to speak with. That is how to be polite on the telephone!

Mobile Manners
(Cell Phones)

See Dick.
See Jane.
See Dick and Jane in class.

Dick is listening to Teacher.
Hear Dick's cell phone ring.
Ring, ring, ring.
Do not answer the phone, Dick!
See Dick sent to the
principal's office.

ell phones can be a good way to keep in touch with your friends and family. But just because you *can* use your phone everywhere, doesn't mean you *should*.

You should only use your phone on your own time or in an emergency. It's also rude to allow your phone to ring in places where it might disturb other people, such as a movie theater or a library. You should always be sure to either turn your ringer off or turn your cell phone off entirely in places like these.

When and Where to Use Your Cell Phone

GOOD		BAD
In your room	*	*In homeroom*
When you're running late	*	*When you're already there*
After a soccer game	*	*While playing a soccer game*
In the lobby during intermission	*	*In the theater during the encore*
At home during a TV show	*	*In church during the sermon*

Instant Messaging

See Jane.
See Jane at the computer.
See Jane typing.
What is she typing?

Jane is IMing with
her friend Susie!
What are those papers
on Jane's desk?
That is Jane's homework,
and she has not done it!

Bad Jane.
Do not talk with your friends
before your homework is done!

*I*nstant Messaging is fun and easy, and a nice way to send notes between friends. But never IM when you need to have an important conversation. If you are going to be late or want to tell your parents you are staying at a friend's house, always call! Remember, typed words often do not convey the same meaning as spoken words. The reader may not get the importance or the humor of what you are saying, so really important things should be saved for face-to-face conversations.

E-mail

See Jane at her computer.
See Jane check her e-mail.
See Jane read a message
from Susie.

Oh my! Susie has invited
Jane to a birthday party!
See Jane reply that she
will be there.
How exciting!

$\mathcal{E}$-mail is a very popular and easy way to stay in touch with friends and family. However, e-mail is not appropriate for every situation. Do not use e-mail for very important conversations that should be held in person.

It is appropriate to use e-mail to catch up with friends, ask quick questions, invite friends to casual social gatherings, and reply to invitations. However, if someone gives you a nice gift, you should send a handwritten note thanking them.

Just because you may be very casual when writing to friends, this does not give you permission to write to adults the same way. Use proper grammar, and always check your spelling before sending an e-mail.

Keeping Safe in Cyberspace

❦

*T*he Internet is one of the great technologies of the modern age. It allows access to information and people from all around the world nearly instantly. You can find an answer to almost any question, and it is available anywhere you have a connection, which nowadays could be as easy as your cell phone!

But the Internet can be dangerous. Just like in real life, there are bad people out there who will pretend to be your friend or even lie about who they are. Never, ever give out personal information on the Internet—this includes your full name, your school, your address, and your phone number.

It is great fun to find Web pages about your favorite subjects and Internet groups that share your interests, whether it is the latest music group or your favorite sports team. You can even find groups for your hobbies, from model-making to beekeeping to playing an instrument. These can be wonderful ways to expand your knowledge and find people who share your interests. Remember that not everything on the Internet is accurate. You should find multiple sources for information, and if something is very important, double-check the information in a book from the library, such as an encyclopedia.

Remember, be safe and keep your information to yourself, and if someone approaches you on the Internet and is not behaving properly, let your parents know immediately. Most of all, have fun and let your imagination grow!

You, Me, and Everyone We Know!

See Dick.
See Jane.
They are on the Internet.
They are chatting with
their classmates.

What are they talking about?
It is a special chat room
for their science class.
They are studying dinosaurs.

Jane loves the triceratops.
Dick loves the T. rex!
ROAR!

*I*nternet chat rooms are places where you can have e-conversations with more than one person at a time. Oftentimes, when you don't see people or hear their voices, it is easy to forget your manners. But as we have learned, we should always have good manners! Shouldn't we?

Use complete sentences as much as possible when typing in a chat room. It is acceptable to use standard abbreviations (see below), but they are not a replacement for good grammar. Remember to respect the ideas of others. You can always disagree, but be friendly and courteous.

Common E-lingo and Definitions

LOL	*	laugh out loud
ROFL	*	rolling on the floor laughing
IMHO	*	in my humble opinion
U2	*	you too
BRB	*	be right back
TTYL	*	talk to you later

Appropriate and Inappropriate E-mails

Appropriate

Dear Susie,

Thank you for inviting me to your birthday party. I would be happy to attend.

Sincerely,

Dick

Inappropriate

Sus . . .

I don't want to come to your party but my mother is making me.

D

*   *   *

Dear Susie,

Thank you very much for the very nice birthday present. I appreciate it very much.

Sincerely,

Dick

Susie—the game you gave me was OK but I am going 2 trade it in for somethin' else.

D

Appropriate

Dear Mr. Johnson,

I would like to apply for the job I saw advertised for the paper route. I am very responsible, I have my parents' permission, and I have my own bicycle with a basket.

Sincerely,

Jane

Inappropriate

Mr. Johnson,

Can I have the job? Doing the paper route. I think it would be kewl and I could use the money. OK?

—Jane

p.s. write me back soon, OK?

*   *   *

Dear Mom,

I am going to be home late. Susie and I will be studying at her mother's house after school for our math exam. Her mother will be home and gave us permission. The phone number is 555-1843.

Love,

Jane

Mom,

I'll be home late. Don't wait up . . . K?

Laters . . . . j

Received an
<u>appropriate</u> e-mail

Received an
<u>inappropriate</u> e-mail

What Have We Learned?

See Dick and Jane eat dinner.
Jane is NOT talking
with her mouth full of food.
Dick is NOT speaking
on his cell phone.

What is Sally doing?
Sally is NOT feeding Spot, even
though Spot is begging for food.

Well done, Jane!
Well done, Dick!
Well done, Sally!

Now you can mind your manners!
Mind your manners, Dick and Jane,
and you will be A-OK!